ALWAYS ASKING MORE QUESTIONS

CLEMENT ROSS

A.K.A. RANGER IGUANA

Library of Congress Control Number: 2025913084

ISBN

978-1-964488-71-4 (Paperback)
978-1-964488-72-1 (eBook)
978-1-964488-73-8 (Hardcover)

Always Asking More Questions

By Clement J. Ross
Aka Ranger Iguana

I dedicate this collection to the following: Lynn Ross (nee Frick), Cyndy Ross, Betty Frick, Gail & Tim Thieman, Jennifer and Mike Jackson, Jan Frick, Morgan Feldhaus, Larry Feldhaus and Patti Frick, Chris Overbaugh, Rebecca Overbaugh, Bob Mooney, Veronica Overbaugh, Ron Lindley, Tanya Lindley, Britt Lindley, Bob & Kitty Mooney, Kitty Shields, Charlotte and Lee Haywood, L.B. and Angelise Boykin, Brad Dumanski, Karen Parker, Michael Steimle, Steve Koleszar, Bea Andrews (RIP), Tim Deegan, James King, Heidi King, Teri Pealer, Frank Smith & Bill Radell (from St. Joes), Mrs. Schaeffer & Mrs. Miller (from Lake Catholic HS), Tim "Teek" Kenneley, Tim "Slick" Miller, Mike Turk, "Rick" Ricciardo, Tom Rosplock, Neil Allen, Catherine Miller & Mrs. Schaefer, Mark Vocca, Mitzi Terry, Lori Terry (RIP), Char Vocca, Tracy Terry, Dennis Terry, Fred and Boo Terry, Doug Enkler, Tom Miller, Frank Smith, Bill Radell, Brandon Zart, Luke Powers, Bill DeGedio, Bob Sablack, Dave Sukys, Jimmy Damm, Connie Tirpak, Suzanne Stiffler, Carol Nieman, Janine Feeney, Jeri Jauch, Missy Sider, Lauren Coyne, Neil Allen, Tom Rosplock, Tim "Teek" Kenneley, Mike Turk, Tim "Slick" Miller, RGR Mike Hall, RGR Howard Mullen, RGR Ronnie Carle (RIP), RGR Rick Knight, RGR Craig Riley, RGR Andrew Lucas, RGR Charles Childers, Reggie Richards III, RGR Roland Crawford, RGR Paul Teigland, RGR Michael Gonzales, RGR Juan Espinosa, Xanthia, RGR Randall H. "Andy" Anderson, RGR Stacy & Karen Nowak, RGR Doug Droesch, Darla Droesch, RGR Eric and Denise Stahl, RGR Dale Kennedy, RGR Huck and Amy Henderson, RGR Marlin Maynard (RIP), RGR Captain

Richard Allen NYPD, Sammie "Jack" & Teresa Sax III, Tim Lindsey, Dean LaVelle, Brian Fee, RGR Marc Leinbach, RGR George Partridge, Micha und Dagi Pauels, Georgio and Fariba Ephraxias, Geneva Foster, Tom Dufty, Klaus-Peter Hinze, Karl Strmn, Louis Brownlowe, Tama Engleking, Jim Frederick, Tom Dufty, Marianne Friend (Schiebli), Suzanna Means, Mike Hudson, Bill DeGedio, Mai Soon Bai, Anna Van Der Meulen with Louis and Alaska, Rebecca Yodi, Sam Petrello, Dave Atkins, Tom Fallon, George Dunn, Dave A. Peterson, Helen "Of Troy" Jenson, Paul Harrigan, Chris O'Connor, Michele Dumaine, John Baer, Kevin and Maureen Hibbard, Wendy Weld, Suzanne Perez, Sandy Hagedorn, Shannon Page, Rich Meyer, Rick & Michelle Jones, Alecia "P!nk" Moore, and Michael Franti.

To those who meant and mean something to me, I salute you all. You know why.

TABLE OF CONTENTS

The Gruesome Verse

ABSOLUTE TRUTHS

Sometimes but not always,
We stumble upon a Möebius strip
And find a truth to call our own.

For the while we stay still,
Our precious truth is safe;
None shall tamper or malign
with cancer streaks of grey.

Even the passersby ignore
This truth whose name they do not know,
As they scurry to find their own.

While standing on this Möebius strip
We faced a choice of next to do…
We found this truth;
Did spare it of harm;
Though none could taint;
There's something wrong…

We watched the sphinx's answer
Becoming one with Cain;
We have this truth, just no keeper,
So we must die in vain.

BALLAD OF THE BOY WITH AMBER EYES

The longest weekend: school-less summer;
neighbor kids would swarm like flies;
In sandlot fields, the games they'd play
like Hooks and Collars, laughs and cries.

As children do, there was that new…
that different kid with amber eyes–
Each pupil like a big black ant,
submerged in honey-syrup tar–
the other kids, why would they want
to share the swings or monkey bars?
And so with rocks and shouts and taunts,
they drove him out beyond the gate.

One Sunday after services,
the gang arrived an hour late;
The diamond taken, they resorted
to kicking frogs and gouging trees,
Until that weirdo boy with amber
eyes appeared along a breeze.
His hair looked mossy, damp and green
…his teeth, as if he'd eaten dirt,
Were black and grey, but how his eyes:
he usually looked sad and hurt.
He tightly held a shoebox un-
derneath his arm; he saw his prey;
He said, "uh, howja like it f'I
would clear that field so you could play?"
And one smug boy responded: "How."
"Like this," he said and showed the box.

An oblong cardboard Keds contain
-er rattling were it full of rocks

Or like a white sepulchre, beau-
tiful but full of dead men's bones—
And then he heard the names again,
antagonistic like the stones
They threw at him—they called him: weir-
do, sissy, bring-a-box, and freak.

He turned and pointed with the box:
the field was empty; none could speak.
The boy with amber eyes then stuck
his hand beneath the lid to grope.
But from within came muffled screals
like abbatoir pigs resigned of hope.
The boy with amber eyes pulled out
his hand to show a fist of worms:
They writhed and strained and one would later
recall in incoherent terms
it almost seemed as if…but weren't
there faces at the ends of them?

Most every boy just could not bear
to watch as he with eyes like gems
Took worms and dirt and stuffed his mouth
—not one disgusted really saw,
Instead they flew that scene and left
alone the boy who grinds his jaw
In circles such to look like chew-
ing—even as the difference between
The truth and fiction must depend
on adolescent memories,
There are now those who would dispute

that something strange occurred that day.

But still two facts remain: the vanished boys who gathered just to play,
And in a field a shoebox waiting for the next weird boy who's willing to pay.

On Bastille Day

Harken upon the sallow whispers
    of spectral souls, the vanquished
wandering in alleys of brick
    and trash for a pause of glances–
as can only be warnings
    of fate if choice relinquished
with accountability ought to pass.
    The last sound shuffling as
knowing not of where return
    takes them weary, too tired to die,
back to hell of paying still…
    Heed the tatters of time's forecast;
what present need not be so far
    and fetched without a care so fast
that numbers of tally tick away
    becoming a blur of indifferent thought.

BITTERSWEET

The bittersweet taste of purple anger
Has carried me on its back;
Then the strength I'd lack
Would rejuvenate with focused danger.

Often amidst will-sapped defeat
Losing then finding myself
Grey with dust on cellar shelf,
Only through anger do I again compete.

With deceit inevitable
From humans so fallible,
My anger's appetite for any just cause
Starves not long before evidence of flaws
Fills me with contempt to justify my sense
Of justice enraged purple and sympathy hence
Has no room on the platform mounted
By my arrogance, my conceit–undaunted.

The bittersweet taste of purple anger
Deceives more frequently than humans,
Leaving partakers in ruins…
Righteously alone for which they did hanker.

Swollen eyes from diseased flies
Cast a famished beam of misty light,
Tracking each intruder.

Could be Libya, could be West 25th,
What really does it matter;
Sadly Biedermeier.

The intruder is a bystander–
A passerby with blinders,
Uninvolved and unashamed.

Once spake Zarathustra…
Yet the recorder's journal for forward thrust
Sits on an antique shelf, collecting dust.

Did Pandora really re-open her box…
Gary Cooper's "High Noon" was just a movie…
Who really wrote *Lunacy Becomes Us*:
The techno-worms of apathy,
Feeding on kinetic energy,
Leaving slime trails of lethargy and rust.

We are plastically sincere
In wonder of shame,
Musing stagnant answers.
We adore our security,
Sacrifice all in her name.

Disney channel hosts "Peter Pan"…
A & E airs "Biedermeier Deutschland"…
What difference lies between the two;
What matter during Biedermeier II?

(Plus ça change, plus c'est la même chose.)

Wir Kinder vom Bahnhof Zoo,
We whore us so blatantly,
We whore us so easily,
All for the fix that has come
To constitute who we are.

The scarecrows never face
The thread held by the ogre,
The thread becoming a lazy noose,
The thread from which they hang
As the ogre heaves a knowing laugh.

Spontaneous combustion never occurs
To any phoenix in never-never land;
More meticulous are the flames
As from within they consume,
Smoldering and gnawing, evermore
Every Scarecrow out-of-place
Without the prayer of rebirth.

We live a fragment. We see narrow.
Randomness and Paradox shan't abandon us:
They've become our new Gods;
They've become our scapegoat;
We are beyond refuge;
We serve their will.

Existing in the Grey Area
Are no longer cynics–
The idealist believing in Black and White
Becomes an adult when he sees the blending
And all that was becomes shades of Grey.

Existing in the Grey Area

Are no longer cynics–
The frustrated idealist turns to reason,
Substituting bygone belief with
That which offers proper answers
In order with the new God's rules
As Chaos laughs mockingly.

Cynics are no longer
Existing in the Grey Area–
The bitter idealist carves a notch,
Wishing sometimes it were his wrist,
reminding of each and every failure;
Anger serves to drive him on empty,
Anger serves to sustain his fever,
Anger serves to drive him over
The edge he fights to cling to.

Remarkably held within a tear,
Cherished between two clasped hands
Is there thus the balance wherein
We find vulnerable still and scarce
A tarnished key made from yule wax,
So easily melted in the listless, dank oneliness,
So easily lit by yet another's wick…
That forgotten notion called compassion.

SEPTEMBER 6, 1989

Thanks to Billy Joel for "Pressure."
Thanks to Lou Reed for "Straw man."
Thanks to Christiane F.
Thanks to Graham Parker for "Another Grey Area."

Dare disturb the darkness

If I as isolation-opting hermit
In deed did naught for fear of freedom,
I'd find me of consequences–unbound.

Dangle death's real danger;
Make it jingle, give it noise;
Keep it like a carrot out in front:
Tantalizing, terrifying,
Giving glints that tear the eye
But don't surprise.

I understand another age,
Enjoyed a life of summer questing:
How might I have this otherwise,
This fired clay both blazed and glazed;
The residue of sins still sticks and stains
When dreams transporting lift and toss–
I want those childhood trees again where safety sat
Up high in limbs that held me sound asleep.

Desperate/daring/deadly/done.

Don't ask do I deserve
whatever wherever I am:
There I am as I delivered me,
Determined but to step and stake
Myself as creator and creation.

Dear Charlie,

Don't be afraid.
The light is coming, not going.
We all love you and want your touch.
    Nothing matters as much.

The next door
Will allow you to enter
Where those you've lost have been found;
    To those shores you are bound.

I weep to lose
The father who took me as his own
But graciously accept this passing
    As a form of fasting

To do without
A nutrient of heart and soul
Until rejoined as we will be
    In the After–your daughter and me.

4/21/2013

For Charlie Frick, my father in law.
A merchant marine in World War II.
A man who meant so much more to me than my own biologically father.

Gail read this poem to Charlie before he passed. Gail is Lynn's sister.

He passed away on April 27, 2013. We miss him so much.

DECAY

Into the grey-clay mass
Nature breathes its breath,
Then gives us over to time
To slowly induce our death.

The stream will animate the stone
And rolling it touches with sentiment,
Until at last it crumbles
As sand returning to sediment.

Decay is a natural course
Which begins at the age
When we profess our arrogance
In public or on a journal page.

"That which does not kill us
Only makes us stronger"
As thought true in my youth,
Now finds my belief no longer.

I've begun to realize
What's long been in motion,
My awareness of decay
Riding the back of emotion,
As I nurture the one
affecting both inadvertently.
But to what ends?
I suspect signs inherently.

"Overload the system
And it will crash,"
Would suit me fine
As an epitaph.

MAY 13, 1992

DOWNTOWN CLEVELAND

The smelting fire, the ash and smoke,
    The throbbing pound and furnace device,
The charnel house, metallic toke,
    The fix became my favorite vice.

The streets are strewn with x-debris
    Among graffiti, tumors grow.
But passion, lust, so desperately
    Both thrive, survive, and fight and glow.

My fact'ry soot collects on sills;
    My nightly noise escapes the rain;
My tab exceeds utility bills;
    My flower pots sustain wolf bane.

The Bridge Street dealers summoned slaves:
    Ohio City's loyal dregs;
And Tremont's art scene has its graves,
    More prominent than Edison's kegs.

So "love" becomes a moment's night,
    A carnal fest of limits broke.
And "love's" a fickle winded kite
    Of back-door offers, fires stoked.

My city stank of emptiness.
    But dreams were 'spose to happen here?
Despite the cringing loneliness,
    I held the reins that I most feared.

    My city bricked the walls above…
    My city brought the grey to clasp…

My city gave the jazz I loved...
My city held me in its grasp...

The city sex was tribal, raw;
    It took untaken willingly:
The yet undone, all named a flaw,
    Until explored so fruitlessly.

My city broke the bounds of one;
    I laid with two in decadence.
My city angered what was fun,
    And took for granted common sense.

The mason's brick can build a wall;
The mobster's tar can fill the road;
The gangster's coin can will a fall;
But what, but love, fulfills abode?

I angst to weep as you've become
    A breathing dying agèd duke,
Defying death, a homeless bum
    In alleys wretching, born to puke,

My city stirs, its craning head,
    It rises born again, not dead,
A beast refusing yet to die:
    As lone as one who loves-but dies,
Or mourns accepting final rest
    My city cheats on every test.

ENOUGH'S ENOUGH

Can you see the face next door?
Can you hear the howling wind?
Can you smell decay and gore?
Do you feel the shape we're in?

There's a lonely fright of quiver'd lips
paralyzed still for a pause of dread;
There's a dog despairing a master's fate
since movement ceased and pool was bled;
There's a leper homeless, dead, diseased,
as fodder for feasting in his sewer bed.

Enough's enough we said and stood
our ground, a stand, misunderstood.

We meant no more we'd take this crap;
"So what?" they said and turned their backs.

We said, "Hey, no wait–this *is* for real"–
They paid no heed to how we'd feel.

And we stood until the dusk came on
then went back home and said so long.

THE GEMINI TWINS

The gemini twins: Regret, Resent,
Stand mute and nod, observing all,
And not atoned, and never lent,
Still waiting since the eden fall.

The first twin plagues and plays with guilt
Imposing subtlety, hints and dues
And makes green flowers wither, wilt,
And madness, sadness-all with clues.

The second ploys with wrath ergo
To tell the toys they're only freed
Defying bitterly the woe
With scorn to banish chains that bleed.

The gemini twins, our shadows long,
Will follow every breath 'til last.
We feed them well to make them strong
Then give them to our children's past.

June 29, 2000

Good Morning, Lover

good morning, lover. rock your hips.
turn and let me kiss your lips.
that telling smile, those eyes ablaze
suggest, to clear the morning haze,
we might unite, and cast off cares;
we should ignite where pubic hairs
entwined and meshed release their sparks,
aromas flood while it's still dark.
and let me pause once fluids flow—
you know just where i want to go:
down to taste your nectar sweet,
down to let my tongue then meet
divinity, its moisture rich,
to savour flavor, to scratch your itch.
divine libations freely flow
and I partake—loving, slow,
promoting ascent, crescendoes build,
exquisitely my mouth is filled.
and then the belly tremors start.
I hold your breast and feel your heart;
it's racing as you clutch my hair,
and pulse and heave, alert, aware,
and then the melting, smooth and still;
you smile with shining eyes until
i look and see your gorgeous face
and wipe my cheeks that bear your taste,
and then we join again as one
and writhe and sweat until the sun
begins to signal dawn's first light,
we grind and focus wrapped up tight

'til cry's release, convulsive throes,
the quaking shudder head to toes,
until the sigh and then a tear;
this woman, whom I love so dear,
as much as I am hers, is mine;
so lucky to have this rose divine.

This one is for Lynn, my lovely wife...

GIVEN THE CHOICE

Coyote caught
will always chew
to its avail.
> *Better to pant than to yawn;*
> *Better to pang than to numb;*
> *Better a rook than a pawn;*
> *Better to lead than to come.*

Mantle relics,
safe and secure,
never worry about their dust.
> *Better to sweat than to sleep;*
> *Better to drive than be swept;*
> *Better to stalk than to creep;*
> *Better alone than be kept.*

Dangled lizard
will separate
from its tail.
> *Better a sponge than a drain;*
> *Better to thrive than hesitate;*
> *Better to seethe than refrain;*
> *Better to try than to wait.*

Weather vanes
turning in winds
never care about their rust.
> *Better a fox than a fowl;*
> *Better a will than a wave;*
> *Better a grin than a scowl;*
> *Better to ash than to grave.*

[Mark said this would make a great jig. I'm not a musician so I take his word for it.]

HAMLET

To be or not to be
Related more to quality
Than intimations of
Suicidality

Aristotle

> *The unexamined life is naught*
> *Nor even worth the premiere spark*
> *Than do to learn, and test, evolve,*
> *or wallow: mushroom moist and dark.*

…how many hollows fill a factory role?
…how many shallows do as each are told?
…how many rejects scatter streets?
…how many outcasts, labeled defeats?

The being begins by disappointing
Expecting ones who patronize
They hold–as if it were a prize–
A mask intended for anointing.

And some succomb and don the face
Allowing it to ebb the former
To dankest depths, forgotten corner,
Until completely gone, erased.

To be or not, a question, choice:
The cryptic query cloaks the threat;
Perhaps it better were a bet–
The damned know well they lost their voice.

The puzzle still lacks definition
No one defines another's "be"
As what it means remains to see
How each brings it into fruition.

The quality to be defined
Without which comes the greying void,
That creeps with stealth and strikes with poise,
Is shaped in dreams we seldom find;

Our human flaws, recalling best,
The nightmares pale that till our soul
So deep in heart where hope could spoil
And trembles trust and brings unrest.

…how many souls are childhood trapped?
…how many victims blamed for crap?
…how many perps are prayed for by
a deathrow mourner forgetting why?

To be or not to be, the quality:
What makes the being have its worth?
What forges meddle, lacked at birth?
What brings the being sanctity?

I've found few answers; questions, more.
What stays, the delving deeper why?
What matters is the will to try
And never quit and pain ignore.

I SING THIS PRAYER...

I sing this prayer for savage souls:
    to all of those by anger caged,
    in bile doused, in acid bathed,
Whose wrath on innocents takes toll.

I sing this prayer for carnal souls:
    who seek perversely flesh depraved,
    and ever unsating objects craved,
Attempt fulfilling harrowed holes.

I sing this prayer for shallow souls:
    who doubt, despair, and cannot cry—
    their barren hopes just break to try
Believing where they feel the pulse.

I sing this prayer for stagnant souls:
    alive in life, in spirit dead,
    apart from heart and trapped in head,
Determined to abide by concrete roles

I sing this prayer for my own soul:
    in thoughts and deeds akin to all
    away from morals, chosing fall;
Let heart alight one path and goal.

IN IT

That power pulses blood and dizzies brain;
I lack the will to summon it alone.
But here, your scent allows a taste of mane
    to conjure dreams in mind though yet unshown.

No feeling in the world compares to this:
No glories, laurels measure 'gainst the glow
Ignited in a whirlwind, taking risk
    to defy the storms that sweep away and blow.

And how a dash suffices in the stew,
The smallest perq propels and charges full
Sustaining 'til the next small dose of you
    that gives my eyes a jolt, my heart a pull:

    Alert, alive and filled: intensity
    That floods the banks of real felicity.

It's About Time

Measure the span
Of how long it took
For you to realize
You were on a hook.

There are no modern gods,
No idols worth the worship;
But you gave relentlessly
As captain on a sunken ship.

Swim to the shore,
stand on the beach;
Now strive like everything
Is just within reach:

Never go home again
To find a closet treasure.
That silly object is a token;
Nostalgia sought for pleasure.

Reel with the wind,
stung by the rain;
Life is worth living
As joy surpasses pain:

For nothing can be known
By living safe and numb;
Growth means pain, as change does fear,
But better than blocking, acting dumb.

"It's about time,"
I said to myself
To practice what I've learned
From my wise book shelf.

MAY 18, 1992

The Lessons Learned

(TEETER-TOTTER STANDING)

I.

The meaning hangs in balance 'tween
Regret. Resent. the demon twins,
Whose eyes see only backward time,
Distracting dawns and yet to be.

The fulcrum holds such symmetry,
The three united sides all same,
A perfect stone, awaiting door,
A ring of brass so far away.

Remaining now amidst the strife:
To look at demons out and in,
To see what sins were mine by choice,
To fight the urge to forfeit trust,
To know the impulse and the just,
And never damn myself again.

II.

I heard such great advice-so why
Did I ignore the words so wise?

When Victor said: just live each day
As if it were a second chance
To live again. Correct the errs
You made before this second pass.

And Victor said: if one does live,
There must then be a suffering
And to endure, the only way
Is finding meaning in the pain.

Then Albert said: that Sisyphus
Was faced with life's futility,
Accepted its absurdity,
Preserving his own dignity.

Then Thomas said: that Prufrock learned
Of minutes where one has the time
For all decisions, revised and made,
Which just one minute may turn astray.

And Andy who led my squad had said:
Remember the six: that prior planning
Prevents (the) piss poor performance–
The best advice prevents the damning.

I heard such great advice-so why
Did I forget the words so wise?

III.

What lies ahead? What next is dead?
What next might thrive? What next might lie?
What else might leech? What might be peace?
The threat, the stain, remain the same.

Inside the ache, the panic fear,
That yet again it could be near,
To give the sky and lose the earth,
Recycled back, await rebirth.

To trust again now after this?

To be the fool and break the bank?
To want the highest with the risk?
To fill the yearning with the right?
To find the path of finally light?

The questions still are those of faith.
Were I to quit the human race
Relinquish all forever more
Or hold the faith for what's in store.

What wasn't wrong was giving trust…
What still was wrong was whom I choose:
Because they were not worth the while,
But more because I didn't suppose.

IV.

I have this guilt from long ago:
I didn't stop the tyrant's blows,
I didn't stop the bully then…
So now compelled the guilt to end:

I walk the streets a lonely man,
Who seeks the comfort of a hand,
Who finds the damaged, others' bled,
Ignoring all the books I've read.

I sought the hero's role in vain,
And soiled my soul with many stains,
The impulse to erase the guilt
And finally sheath my sword to hilt.

So turn now face the changes strange,
Said David with his voice in pain;
And meet tomorrow grasping just,
Just like the man called Sisyphus.

V.

– Santayana

Returning to the ambush site,
Amidst the mocking of the Twins,
Who pour the salt and rub it in,
I see the shards & teeth that bite.

Illusions fallen, broken, dead
That once were home and role and life,
With mortgage, debts, two cars and wife
…just like a bullet in the head.

And now the wasteland's barren, free,
But still the signs remain: facades
Reflected in the broken shards
Of former struggles pathetically.

Examining the parts once whole,
Ignoring taunts of demon twins,
I focus on my role and sins,
Where I went wrong to salvage this soul.

I fully gave trust, despite the doubts,
Believing when the reason was naught,
Relinquishing all but ought,
And volunteered for a one-way route.

How much was love of love a part
Which blinds the seeker trading self
So eager into love to delve;
Inevitably, the cost is heart.

Remember yearning, passion, thrill
To stave off jading, cynic's defeat;
Remember impulse grants repeat
Of choosing that which won't fulfill.

I leave the wasteland at memory's door,
Returning to the present day;
The sky ahead still purple grey,
I shake my head but still want more.

I'm not dead yet; this self, intact.
I'll find another–this time true
And give and get as both are due
And make a home: no mirrors cracked.

June 18-29, 2002 – Patti created this one.

Liquid Lear

I want to be a jelly sac
to be like Gloucester' s eyes
Plucked out from life and then discarded
if I can't see the earnest lies.

So down then down
this deadly doom
So down to where the base and seed
fail to thrive entombed.

Let rain erode the hardened plane
Let torrents split the level stone
Bring back the dirt and muck unclean
and bury there a Yorick bone.

And yet today I see them still
and mark tomorrow in a prayer
until that when of truth as ill
then let me under earth to lair.

Some of these like this one wrote themselves.

LULLABYE

Tranquil madness overwhelms
the conscious subject will
and "those little slices of death"
taking their turn to reign,
as one by one layers of
Resistance are stripped off
like dead skin from a burn victim,
evince a foreign victor.

Tranquil madness renders
the conscious subject will
helpless as the cribbed infant
whom the eager rat awaits,
patient as time's pendulum grazing
–sliver by sliver–
that firm control defense
as easy as plucking fingertips.

Hand over the scepter of power to Id unbound,
free as Prometheus yet without his credo,
and Dare not any cognizance during this despot's reign
for chance to witness the soul's dark Zeitgeist.

Requiescat in pace is a lie;
for indeed all noble virtues and sentiments
are replaced with the history of guilt
in deed and thought by the observers
Regret and Resent, omniscient yet silent,
until the still succumbing at night.

Fall with a whimper, not a sigh,
and remember the prayer of forgetfulness.

Edgar Allen Poe called sleep, "those little slices of death."

M'AIDEZ, MAY DAY

A crash, the bottom slams—cold and dank,
What world above below the pit?
My chest is cold. Within the well, my heart,
So deep in dank…and madness overhead.

The slip inside where none may prod or peek,
Such lookers-on just sneer and scoff that here
I hide so safe within the shell of blank;
They never see the screals, the cuts, the dice

that roll each time with ones, the eyes of snakes,
that once—but now, the venomn climbs my veins
until my head, this gourd, so hollow, waits
for push to blank the thoughts that writhe like worms

who feast on corpses left to die alone;
and yet these thoughts are panged with hunger stark
unsated, screaming at the walls around
this tomb enscribed with mottos, crests,

A shrine awaiting final rest—undone.
My darkness cries unanswered from the geist
that drives me mad with reasons blue and sound,
and green and such, I touch a nothingness

and find its call, its song, a tune I know,
familiar sweet and somber notes are night
and moon and dark and howls and graves and tears;
the things that being here are all about.

The anger's blood is scarlett hot and melts
the purest hearts without remorse and then

would seek to damn the innocence from spite;
they dare to dash the hope to unclaimed dust.

The arrogance would take the lame and break
each bone and condescend with every snap
that none were good enough to remain
a fragile piece that might have grown so whole.

The wrath becomes an overwhelming cloud
enveloping grey, those both the good and bad
and everybody in-between until
they breathe the deathly cloud and die of fumes

and stupid people do these heinous deeds:
your priest, your cop, your saint, your planted seeds.
I sit in madness all around, a clown, a freak,
I am the two and yet I seek
to find the shelter underground
where logic, sanity are bound
to show their long dead heads.
and somehow salvage all the dreads…

But that is not reality.
And so I wait for harmony,
A vessel through this tortured land,
until I find that beach of sand

where wide awake, each there'll be
surroundings of mere sanity.
Until that day, I may be grim
because it's such a selfish whim.

MAY 3, 2002

MASQUERADE

The bassett-hound man looking like
a mechanic in December was beaded
in muddy sweat of dank summer steam
as he held his cup for coinage pleaded.

The tailor-suited manager whose brow
seemed even higher with his grey receding
hairline result of what better life with
his porsche at thirty and a wife for breeding.

Passing by the dumpster path between 4th & 5th,
Par-man heard a voice that posed, "Spare any change?"
Prior par of choices always had determined
past response to channel scope and range.

Except today he rendered coins quite eagerly,
and dropped them into waiting palms;
    alas, afraid
to change though knowing not why he'd spare
as coins through holes in palms
    did pass: charade.

MENTOR, OH

Remember the thick forest we called,
"The Woods," and how as Tom and Huck
A whole day meant golden treasure hunt,
Wild beast tracking, up in trees stuck,
Pathfinders exploring, a daredevil stunt,
And talk of bold ideas as time just lolled.

Then the Woods became our Walden…
Less a pair of banded rogues,
We ventured for solitude and repose;
We never joined the crowd en vogue;
We needed this sanctuary–I suppose
As most teen boys thinking we were wise men.

We grew up alright;
But we grew up all white.

…white as the linen of fifties' Moms;
…white as the face of Authority figures;
…white as the picket fence painting our palms;
…white as the jokes about sex, about "niggers."

So we grew up tight
And we narrowed the white.

…white as the bib of the Alter boy gown;
…white as the heal enraging repression;
…white as the bulb before it's blown;
…white as the page before the impression.

As we waited for a fight,
It happened over night.

What happened to our Woods is no personal crime;
There is a demand for suburban facades.
So they chartered our territory, chopped and cut;
They broke all our trees and laid plastic sod;
They poured concrete plazas for consumers' glut.
Now we toast to them—please pass the lime.

Apologies for the N-word. I truly hate it. Moreso because so many people used it when I was growing up as if it were common place and accepted, understood as a given. That's so wrong.

METAMORPHOSIS

The worm I was...
> did not seek the sun's warmth;
> writhed away from touch or tear;
> sought the safe and murky clay;
> dug the hole deeper, dug the grave;
> and shut off emotion, out of fear.

The cocoon I am...
> is on the verge, beginning to know;
> is battered by the wind and rain;
> clings to my flower's stalk,
> clings like moss to stone;
> hides me inside pulsing slow;
> may opt to die with the drain;
> shows a shell, not yet dead,
> waiting in dread
> of changes unknown.

What I will become...
> eludes my voice;
> could flit in skies of fame;
> could incinerate with selfish name;
> remains my choice;
> balances between can and want;
> begins at night to haunt–

So falls the fate of my condition
between potential and its fruition.

Inspired by Bowie's song "Quicksand."

MODERN ART

So as elitist snob of modem art,
I see the costly framed displays of "works,"
Dividing each respectively in part:
 Aesthetic masters or the pencil clerks.

When viewed and understood, you feel the change,
Intuit something previously unknown–
And this is art, exploring some new range;
 And we derive a pleasure, what is shown.

But look upon a canvas colored without
The feeling necessary for response;
The only sense acquired is nagging doubt
 About the "talent" here the dabbler flaunts.

 Theirs may be called a graphic image–But!
 Don't call it art: that's far too deep a cut.

What heals the heart, what soothes the soul?
What Frankl found one night so cold,
Along the march midst dread and strife,
The vision he saw was his own wife:
This Auschwitz inmate grasped the goal
That holds the greatest meaning in life;

That gives oppressed the nerve to dissent;
That grants the weary guts, intent–
Enduring like wolves, together in dens,
Who mate for life, so loyal, intense,
With passion of lovers, exhausted and spent,
whose glances are signal to pulling again.

The answer is neither in Kant nor Locke,
Nor Testament gift from shepherd to flock;
The answer's a prize, fought for and won
And earned again daily, to never be done.
All else is naught, including the clock,
If never resign, and head on we run.

Victor Frankl wrote "Man's search for meaning."

What really matters…
What makes a difference,
has significance, has meaning
    in this slice of reality to which I am witness…
Within this fraction,
subjective noesis can never surmount to becoming the actual…
        Futility reigns…
        the rearing hood
        striking at the hand
        reaching for the gem.
        Futility reigns…
        the gold-green scales
        coiled so smugly
        taunting with hypnotic sway-
As I perceive, I filter
in order to take this grey dank world
    and paint it, giving it more,
    making it palatable.
As I transcribe, I delude,
As with any withdrawal
from the account of truth:
    I put it in a side show
    then pointing fingers, call out, "Freak."
        Look into this cage…
        Within it I've placed
        a Panther and a Hunger artist.
        Look into this cage;
        how they one
        another assunderate.
        It's the only choice left
        and then they die.

We must control
what little we have left of a world to call our own
    even if it means destroying it…
For that one moment
we shall feel revelry
    in senseless waste and death.
        Curiosity of death
        leads the boy's clumsy fingers
        to tear off a leg with the wings
        and then in the pencil well
        back and forth
        stabbing at each exit.
How good to watch a being die,
to watch the living suffer and expire.
Just to blink with tense jaw muscles
…knowing it's not me this time
…knowing I'll numb to belief
that a shell is not a person.

With respect to Rainer Maria Rilke and Franz Kafka.

JULY 10, 1991

Old Cocoons

Dig deep down,
Grope in the dark
To find the buried treasure
And bring it to the Light.

Retrieve the little box
That burns the finger tips
Without knowing if it's
Icey grey or blazing white.

Pull slowly…
Lest the haste
Should cause the object
To dissipate.

As the form
Takes its gradual shape,
Less opaque the nearer
Drawn to the heart,
Still the trembling hand.

Open the eyes;
Unclench the fist.
The tyrant worm
Was after all
A monarch, orange and black
Like a halloween costume
Innocent beneath the mask.

Though memory clouds
With fear, apprehensive
Remains the miner

Even after the butterfly
Ascends, free and away.

Old cocoons in which
Memory hides the worms
Need only be sought
And brought into the Light.

JULY 31, 1991

1950s...

The "Wild Ones" in their leathers black,
And denim blue, and Harley caps,
The maids they left "in a family way"
And lived carefree, more search of prey.
The swingers, Hef & more, were hip:
Dug jazz, the nazz, and smokes and lips
And connessieured their opposites
Who savored putting on the ritz.

1960s...

The BCPs for middle class
Allowed the hubbies much more ass;
Affairs aplenty while their wives
Sought their own joys from too-dull lives.
While youth dissent was different then
(their parents on the fringe again);
Free love, do drugs, commune and groove
But what did any really prove?

1970s...

What did the "Revolution" mean?
The free-lance license each club scene:
The beegees fever disco tramps
Or purple mohawk punkrock vamps.
So prevalent was apathy:
"I'll fuck whomever carelessly"
And once again with the malice
Came "Bob & Ted & Carol & Alice."

1980s...

Then suddenly with herpes, A.I.D.S.
Reducing parties and parades
The safe were celibate or wed
And sex caused fear and filled with dread.
So telephones became the line
To breach and fill the blue divine
Like Blondie's "Call Me" song invite.
A chance to walk with voice delight.

1990s...

With both the het'ro and the gay.
A "bareback" ride becomes the way
To disregard, ignore the chance
Of STDs from limbo dance.
Menage à trois and orgies back,
Or cyber sex through modem jack,
With piercings, goth, and S &M,
At fetish clubs with raising hem,

Year 2000...

A decade new and what remains
To fill the public with disdains?
What's left to overdo, exploit?
What feat remains yet unemployed?
The thrills are gone: no more taboos.
No inhibitions left to lose;
So then perhaps a quest anew:
To seek "true love;" so overdue.

29 JUN 00

TO PANDORA

If was not–had never been
And sights of mind–never seen,
I'd leave the limits to this plane
And live quite dead although insane.

If unreal could never exist
And fact imposed on no resist,
I'd let shell fall, and let ghost give
Up and out where seethers live.

If in mind no corners kept
And all the light just shone and leapt,
I'd leave this lair: down through the drain
Then venture to the dark's domain.

How this pang unearths the driven;
To each a spark so gladly given.
Make wide each box for humans' sake
To reign and falter wide awake.

THE PORTRAIT

The portrait of God was down in the cellar,
Some re-sale shop on West 25th.
Its frame contained official papers
dispelling all the popular myths.

The figure displayed in oil once brilliant
Was aged so gray, so dorian over span
Of time allowing dust and decay,
The portrait had lost appeal to man.

Not even a scribbled name was drawn
Inviting collectors' compulsive mirth;
And previous critics had panned the piece
As amateur: without aesthetic worth.

How I was drawn to pause and hold
That gaze indicative of loss and guilt
As if the eyes knew such regret
From swords left sheathed up to each hilt.

The last I'd heard, the dealer's store
Was headlined as an arson case:
Insurance fraud to settle a debt
And write it off as negligible waste.

A Prayer for Dignity

Appealing path of least resistance,
where comfort lies–keep my distance.
To live, to suffer, equated thus:
the cost at stake, my worthiness.

Gods of heaven, saints of Earth,
this coward since the date of birth
could not taste pain without such fright
and overwhelmed, chose hasty flight.

Gods of heaven, saints of Earth
help this mortal grasp the worth.
Moments fleeting, hours slip 'way,
once again this need to pray.

Not for answers, nor a cure,
these are mine to seek, endure.
In desperation, hanging on,
a plea for help to keep me strong.

Sex and the Single Victim
(ATTN: Boys Only)

You lounge and watch:
"a XXX-er slassher, part II of VI"
Wide eyes sponge, soaking up
Blonde bionic bimbos, pink of panties
...some are braless under the T
...some bikinied, wet with steam;
And in your heart,
you gleam, for all
will fall...

                    !Surprise!

The demon springs up throbbing!
He's wicked, he's heavy, he's
F/X hours with condom latex.
The demon lunges, her belly!
It oozes; It's bloody; It's
F/X hours with crimson cream.

Sensual screams: Pseudo-defense.
Feel your heart race (that look on her face,
her tender thigh loin), the ache in your groin.
What a head rush! Now is your chance:

Let loose a howl.
Be one with the night.
It's only a movie,
that makes it all right.

SHADOW ESSENCE

Mankind is the obstacle
The soul must overcome
To release with unity,
No more hiding from…

Magic Mirror bending
Show me please once more
The glimpse that holds the essence,
The shadow of my soul.

The one who spares my sleep
By making haunts less stark,
Compelling dread to don
A symbol costume cloaking
In mystery doubt of seeming threat,
But not the sinister element.

How much through which
Frail humans may survive
Remains so grey in our minds.

The shadow essence pities,
Paternalistic and knowing
More about the self than we.

Thus it waits for us to choose,
To make our move as one brave soul
And face our fears—just like the diver
Leap   up and out.

THE THIN GREEN LINE

Euthanasia, self-defense,
Guilty-conscience suicide;
In accord with common sense,
Some deserve that final ride.
Rapist and the child molester
Disembodied, slow and cruel;
Fitting end for spineless cur
Justifies the means' renewal.

Humans have capacity
To commit atrocity
And still remain humane,
If the cause be worth the gain.

New York Shuffle Training Camp:
Lies while looking in her eyes;
Let the diaper stay so damp;
Standing by while someone cries;
Close the door with no remorse;
Do the act for selfish need;
Rotting carrots lead the horse;
Blinders are the blocker's greed.

Monsters have capacity
For unthinkable atrocity
By blocking the affect
On emotions they reject.

Can I be this paradox?
Between my feet, the thin green line,
Within my soul, Pandora's box;
Can choice defy innate design?

UNBURNED

I am not long-for this world.
My flag was short to be unfurled.
A spark that flared, then embered dim;
"Who would remember him?"

I ranked with none, with whom compare,
Few lived as I would only dare.
Alone in life: so filled to brim,
"Who would remember him?"

My soul's at war with consequence.
Regret, resent, and all that since,
To stay alive, my chance is slim.
"Who would remember him?"

I weep in darkness; though in light,
I stand my ground, no fear of fight;
Where is my tree, that sacred limb?
"Who would remember him?"

The devil dares not come with pact:
I know the truth, how he'd react;
For what he gave; and naught returned…
Who would remember him unburned?

THE VERGE

When standing on the border line
Between the nations, friend and foe,
Distancing the hostile side–
Not always simply walking fro.

See the verge as mobile;
As imminent, its approach.
Lacking linear evasive route,
Begins the realm, its encroach.

When standing at the passageway
Of neither option convinced,
Wishing won't relinquish choice
And God's become just too distanced.

The longer the debate
Of true preferred plateau,
The stronger feeling of feeding pulse–
The brink's growing shadow.

MAY 22 & 28, 1992

VENERY

Smell the stew, the marinaded flesh
    Moothing with rhythmic heaves;
Simmering to gasp release
    Between four posts as sleeves
And folds mesh and stir the oblong
    Vessel porously sharing and taking
Part in exchange of sucking broth
    And oozing froth during baking.
Meter of thermal intensity metronomes
    Higher sliding further down; some
Verving as the beef-scented soup
    Bubbles toward pending freedom.
A feast of moist velour blending
    With substance and steam as part
Of a unique whole, fluidly lithe
    In creation of traditional art.

WAITING TO READ

I walk along the step by step,
Unsure of words, with doubt, inept.
Where reason cites, I blank reply
    But being speechless burdens why.
There is a lie in comfort zones:
Those peaceful now high-interest loans;
The cost thereafter staggers such
    The fall may prove a bit too much.
So not to seek the platitudes–
Instead to wait for healthy foods;
And so to fast with naught to read,
    Instead of blinders, bags of feed.
But still the burning hunger stark
For gospel prose to pierce the dark
Exists without some respite which
    Might balm or soothe this gnawing itch.
At night the sharpest pangs increase
When active echoes steal the peace;
But then to sleep, relinquish sighs,
    Accept escape as angst subsides.

THE WALL

O core where sank this ship of fools,
A somewhere screams, an elsewhere dreams,
Arena all around with rules
Unheard, unknown, no seeds to glean.
O depth in which the sinking dank,
What flames were doused, what passions lost,
The verve, the drive, the thralls: they sank,
They spilled like chalice blood; same cost.

O what became divinity?
Or was it all along a lie?
No haven for the sanity
Awaited with a hopeful cry.

I wonder why the autumn trees
Will lose their means and winter die,
And then they'll spring with phoenix breeze:
While we're the same-I don't know why.
And here the bricks are blue and tall;
I see the stars and bars and fall
To crawl the distance to the wall–
Until I see no doors at all.

2002

WE PASSENGERS ON BOARD

All aboard the trolley,
Sleepy yawn, a folly,
Lolling plod, a flit in a gust,
And onward rolls the tourbus.

Just like you, me myself
I sought a seat on antique shelf
 & compete collecting residue and dust

…and onward rolls the tourbus.

How we adore security:
No sacrifice too big of me
In shameless wonder casting blame
Like skipping stones, a stakeless game.

…and onward rolls the tourbus.

Thus to justify our deeds,
We never mind a god who bleeds;
We choose what fits the narrow mold
 & trim the excess as we're told.

The road so narrow lies ahead
And someday yet, we shall be dead.
But safely belted in the seat,
No threat from thought we can't delete.

…and onward rolls the tourbus.

… you can't create or destroy energy–
it can only be changed into something else.

paraphrasal of a quote believed to be from Sir Isaac Newton

"Gutta cavat lapidem, non vi sed saepe cadendo."

(The drop of rain maketh a hole in the stone, not by violence, but by oft falling.)
Latimer, 7th Sermon before Edw. VI, 1549
– Ovid (43 B. C. • 18 A.D.?)

I.

Do tales of poltergeister come to mind?
Do humans so disturbed they couldn't let go
Of this–a prize, a love, whatever–find
themselves obsessive presences of woe?

Before they died, we had the chance to show
Through Kirlian photography some proof;
but inconclusively the answer: no,
defining facts remain unseen, aloof.

But who then watches over sleep and paints
The nightmares symbol-safe, and cloaks the fears-
Deliberately to intervene! What saints
have heeded, shown such mercy sparing tears?

The concrete proof for souls and saints remains
evinced in teary prayers and pillows stained.

II.

"und was kommt jetzt wird anders sein.
O kommt es denn!"

...and as the recently Dead, we dare not greet
the mourners at our service– family, friends
whose love ensures our passage, verily
    releases us to join the others; whence

belonging to the party veiled in white
and yes we did survive– although there's more:
the garden flowers, memories, spread wide
    and bloomed forgiveness neither feigned nor

distorted– fully grasping, rendering one
without a hindering fear– to reach this plane
and fully thrive, alive! alive! oh wonder
    could conceive the garden we would gain.

    Come join us once disguises freely fall;
    'til then we'll wait– the readiness is all.

III.

Give me no more contemptuous glances
Nor the sneers: for did they not rejoice
The Fall of Berlin's Wall– such chances
    As in Eden still occur; for choice

And consequence inherently are linked:
It wasn't a Fall– but liberation– for
Naively ignorant & indistinct
    The Blissful still in paradise: such a bore!

Without the knowledge "fruit" bestowed: guess what?
No ethics at all & everything goes
 & nothing's better than anything else:– but
    So commonplace & so mundane… suppose

    That I, the serpent, first of Angels, was
    Heroic bearing eternal blame & cause.

IV.

MEMO FROM THE ACCTG DEPT.

MY DEAREST CLERGY: empty chairs are costing.
So modestly proposed—let's offer formal
Soul Absolving: have our cake and frosting,
    but push the profit margins black to normal.

There'll be complaints—that crimes like rape, molesting
a child, assault, and others against a person
where victims are involved—from those detesting
    this way we'd paint the past a prettier version…

It would behoove decisioning leaving off
the mentioning: "long-term effects" and those
affected (if there needs be talk: use soft
    and gentle words, and try to blow the nose,

    and dab the eye—at certain moments, of course).
    I thank you for your time. SINCERELY YOURS…

V.

The Watcher waits until the REMs subside;
The boy was going to dream about the rape:
When he was seven, sleeping over, cried–
    His best friend's older brother, mouth agape.

The Watcher paints the scene with symbol dust
To spare the sleeper starkest truths of past
Experience too cruel to handle just
    As mem'ries, lost and painful, blocked at last.

The Watcher weighs, deliberates which acts
May be allowed to slip and rise as dreams
And which are too severe when gruesome facts
    Might live again with anguish, dread, and screams.

    Will death unite us with this patron who
    In life and sleep watched over me and you?

VI.

As devil's advocate, I want to play:
So Newton said we can't destroy this "it"-
This energy which animates the clay,
    that glows as long as candles stay alit.

And when they're snuffed: what then? Evaporate
Becoming particles in clouds that pour?
Or like a scattering, just dissipate
    atomically too small to view or store?

Or could the clay itself entomb the spark
Inert, inactive, trapped within the core
Immobile, angsting out the wait through dark
    eternity, controlling nevermore–

    but then again, it might just fly: and free
    become a form we can't yet know or be.

VII.

Not standard costume–beatnik black beret-
Nor angst-deprived artistic ennui,
Conveys contempt for all-the-rage per se,
    but under pretense of intensity

Adhering to the uniform code of spit:
Bohemian conduct in attitude and dress
For then contrived feigning would be legit-
    except for bourgeois tastes–no don't confess

If shared…must never be shown. 0 Modern Artist,
The most elite of souls alive, create:
Aesthetic image suggesting Picasso's cubist
    phase, thus enhancing civilization, fate

    and life–if only we'd been there instead
    of watching late night T.V. while in bed.

VIII.

*When belief in a god dies
the god dies. —Seal of Solomon*

Belief: divine abstraction…followed, willed
Intangible—for all we know, illusion—
Faith, but pure! And God, how joyous, fulfilled
    are those of doubt devoid and spared confusion.

Devotedly sure, convinced that truth makes fact,
Their hearts the source of proof that truth requires:
Defy abstract—from context fact extract—
    thus act: illogic lets them live unmired.

Security wrap us snug and warm… there has
To be hereafter something greater, worth
The wait—and how the heart knows God en masse
    because it wants and needs it after earth.

    But what if unfulfilled and unconsoled,
    if nothing after leaves us rotting mold?

IX.

The Lord is my salvation; He (and then
I have to pause–tradition says it's "He"
But what do I believe?) is listening when
 I pray at night (and I assume this me

Is so important to God), observes my acts
Most every day (I never see a trace
Of proof), and guides me (when empirical facts
 Might cast the plastering shadows over my face).

Such comfort is the God I don't know how
I ever could live without true faith therein
(The mere suggestion, prospect, won't allow
 Considering reality wherein

 Finality of death is true and factual);
 We only get one shot at life that's actual.

X.

Become a ghost, a choice: if focused will,
Determination, keeps one still on Earth
With heaven to a soul, a whale to krill,
    A better place than Hell, and yet its worth

Misunderstood, mismeasured, made the second
Choice for spectres still inhabiting homes;
However, now consider what has beckoned,
    Is just enough for one who stays and roams.

If strong enough is faith that once expired,
That after living another form remains,
The mist of memories, feelings furnace fired,
    Evaporates, transformed intact into remains

    Anew, this non-material energy:
    But still the question, is there harmony?

XI.

I give you thus these words from God and pray
That each abiding listener takes such heed
That not a worry nor a doubt delay
    Our making this reality in deed

And thought for heaven's sake, so listen well:
"Now Thou Shalt go to church and not forget,
Lest ye deny *for* whom tolls the steeple bell;
    And Thou Shalt worry not of cost and debt

And Thou Shalt pledge to give a monthly sum;
And Thou Shalt offer pious servile corpus
without complaint as though thou wert but dumb
    And Thou Shalt make in readiness thine orifice–"

    (I guess I went too far) But give or take
    A few details, was cogently a choice awake?

XII.

In love with death, interred with lust, luxurious;
In lieu of life and letting live, I'll take
A death, deliberate and furious,
 And die delightfully for Phoenix' sake.

Don't bother with coercion, coaxing or
Convincing me–I know about it all.
I can't stay young–I won't grow old before
 This deed–decay's the thing I cannot stall.

Abiding by the ancient code and why
Then Socrates the Hemlock drank, if law's
Accepted, then I must remain and die
 A withering gust, a geist indifferent and flawed.

 And so I take my leave and bid adieu
 And pray (my God!) that God is real and true.

XIII.

"And in the house light after light
Went out, and I was all alone,

A hunger seized my heart; I read"

While everyone else had gone to bed
    The last to leave the library believed
    That later needs must be retrieved
The memory of the words he'd read,

The songs and stories so well loved
    And shared with those asleep below;
    He mem'rized each and knew by rote,
Reciting late at night and oft

Refused to let his sleep erase
    The memories of the tales and songs;
    Admittedly there'd be along
With sleep the dreams of time and place

    All new–but neither to replace
    nor let the lyrics become effaced.

XIV.

The struggle, search to cross the human bars
through which the hands may grope but nothing seize
from out the veil so blank and grey: a farce?
 …not long ago mere promises appeased.

Who know are only those who cannot say,
And yet communicate they do—soft hints,
Allowable signals, blatant haunts convey
 Detail suggesting all the shades and tints.

"There's no such thing as truth; there're only facts,"
A wise old mentor said and startled me
To thought about my questioning and acts
 Attempting to convince myself there'd be:

 A genuine proof I could unearth and dearly
 Hold in heart:—if nowhere else as nearly.

XV.

I'll sing to touch, connect to all that thrive
and seethe outside myself instead of in;
I'll give not take and hope becoming wise
    results, rewarding one who used to sin.

Through faith and hope and charity, I may
yet through a glass so darkly see the light
and know in heart the dawn of every day
    is splendrously renewing, though the night

was spent amidst these stones and flowers fenced;
but here where shells are brought and buried deep,
the only feelings ling'ring felt and sensed
    are mourned remainders, not from those asleep.

    So call the carcass but a shell without
    emotive residue of fear and doubt.

XVI.

My faith in reason holds that God's a lie:
In desperate times, in dank despair, I'd not
Expect the master's voice to answer why.
    But disappointed, rest my case, as ought.

If true, were not the opportunity
The perfect chance to prove default a must,
Should one exist-the possibility
    Must lend itself as reasonable and just.

So where's the offer? Where to sign my name?
"The readiness is all"-a spoiled chance.
No brimstone, teasing, luring, contract, fame,
    And I was ready, baited breath, to dance.

    Were Satan real, there'd be a bargain done;
    Without the other, either must be none.

XVII.

And Newton, nature clued the seeker thus;
The evidence I quarrel to and fro.
Like Isaac found in grains of sand and dust
    That purpose, therefore, proof of God and soul.

I angst before this claim and sadly yet
I can't deny the proof that nature shows:
Accept, allow my heart with no regret,
    Defying logic? How? Somehow it knows.

There was a time I fought the notion of
A soul or God because I could, I stood
So firmly bent on havoc first, not Love,
    I had to open up my mind to Good.

    I must rethink my past, my history.
    But Bible still remains a mystery.

It's true. God is real and so are souls.

NOTES:

SONNET II

Das Buch der Bilder by Rainer Maria Rilke
poems from a seven-year life: June/ 899 to Augusl 1906

"ln weißen Schleiern gehn die Konfinnanden
tief in das neue Grun der Garten ein.
Sie haben ihre Kindheit uberstanden,
und was jetzt kommt, wird anders sein.
O kommt es denn!"

DIE KONFIRMANDEN (PARIS, IM MAI 1903)

(ln white veils the confirmed enter
deeply into the new green of the garden.
They have survived their childhood,
and what comes now will be something changed.
So let it come!)

SONNET XI

" And in the house light after light
Went out, and I was all alone,
A hunger seized my heart; I read"

– Alfred, Lord Tennyson from *In Memoriam A.H.H.* Lyric #95

THE GRUESOME VERSE

A IS FOR ANGUISH

What do you feel…
when the shadows creep?
when you cannot sleep?
when footsteps follow?
when walls are hollow?

What do you feel…
when all is narrow?
when card's are tarot
and death occurs
but it's not the worst?

What do you feel…
when dark is loud?
when luck's a shroud?
when sleep's not safe?
when light's a wraith?

What do you feel…
when all closes in?
when life's a sin?
when breath is tight?
when nothing's right?

What do you feel…
when corner's stone
but seems like home;
your back is cold
and wet with mold?

What do you feel…
when you're all alone

when heart is stone
when soul is ice
and thoughts so vile can now entice
and all that is
is was and not to be:

How well can you say
you still can see?

B IS FOR BLACK

It's darkness, dread; it's *The Unknown.*
It's shadow, night; it's raven's wing.
It's mourning shade; it's *all alone.*
It's lurking like a scary thing.
...the stain on white;
...the cause of fright.

The bulb burned out; the attic view.
Beneath the bed; the woods at dusk.
It fills the sky long after blue.
The scent beyond the cellar's musk.
...the void of light;
...the blind man's sight.

It paints the grave beneath the ground.
Sublime and luring, deep, profound.
It arcs around a vampire's eyes.
It taints the hue of bold-faced lies.
...it's stormy clouds;
...it's bell-toll shrouds.

C IS FOR CATALOG OF CREEPS

A child molester on parole;
A greedy jerk who sold his soul;

The "I'm with stupid" t-shirt wearer;
The alley lurking bosom starer;

The cyber slob young teen coercer;
The terrorist bombing plot-rehearser;

The hiding coward who later lies;
The adult arcade pervy guys;

The angry drunk who beats his wife;
The sadist torturing with a knife;

The virus making 'puter geek;
The predator upon the meek;

The renegade rapist on the loose'
The football star known once as "Juice;"

The parish priest who likes young boys;
The NAMBLA members seeking joys;

The altar desecrating cad;
Abusers making children sad;

This list has more
But that might bore
Or start a war.

So avoid each one,
Or take a gun
And have some fun.

D IS FOR DEMON

From Hell it came, the hornèd beast,
Upon the human flesh would feast:
It loves what rots, decays, is dead;
It's scaly, hairy, sometimes led
By chains unless it should attack
With hunger, thirst for bloody snack
Devoured whole, or piece by piece;
It loves the living best deceased.

It eats its victims' bone and flesh,
Then spreads it wings, like iron mesh,
And shrieks a scream of victory
Alerting all of sanctity:
A soul's been damned, and angels weep.
Another lost we couldn't keep.

•••

I met a demon whose quota fell–
It sought the evil souls who'd dwell
On sins that should have been
Mere youthful foibles–never "sin."
And *all* his lies luring tricks achieved
Damnation quick yet who'd've believed?

For Someone said, *"Enough's enough…
That's not akin to sinful stuff."*
The demon wept reptilean tears;
Fulfillment came to all its fears:
The redefining of what is just
And what it sin, as so it must:

In hell, they dropped the demon's rank
To flatulation sniff of stank.

The everyman will mow his lawn;
The everyman will pull the weeds;
The everyman will greet the dawn;
The everyman will plant his seeds.

The everyman will smoke his pipe;
The everyman will drown his pain;
The everyman will harbor gripes,
The everyman will go insane.

The everyman will trumpet loud;
The everyman will kill the snake;
The everyman will join the proud;
The everyman will shortly wake.

The every man will mute restraints;
The every man will seek new balm;
The every man will hear false saints;
The every man will quench the calm.

The everyman will stain the white;
The everyman will breech the womb;
The everyman will start the fight;
The everyman will find the tomb.

The every man will seek his muse;
The every man will masturbate;
The every man will read the news;
The every man will celebrate.

The every man will shed a tear;
The every man will beat his dog;

The every man will sate each fear;
The every man will be a cog.

The every man will hate his life;
The every man will fantasize;
The every man will beat his wife;
The every man will spurn the wise.

The every man will read bad books;
The every man will hope for loss;
The every man will be mistook;
The every man will love the frost.

The every man will dominate;
The every man will torture cats;
The every man will insinuate;
The every man wears many hats.

The every man will notice curves;
The every man will thrust a knife;
The every man will deaden nerves;
The every man will fuck your wife.

The every man will pedophile;
The every man will magnify;
The every man will lack no style;
The every man will deify.

The every man will be distinct;
The every man will reach beneath;
The every man will love instinct;
The every man will sharpen teeth.

The every man will disco dance;
The every man will play with guns;
The every man will stain his pants;

The every man will sicken nuns.

The every man will die awake;
The every man will join the mad;
The every man will good forsake;
The every man could be your dad.

F IS FOR FRANKENSTEIN

The castle high drew no more light,
Despite the sun's proximity,
Than any grave's silent night
Or the crypt's hallowed sanctity.

But deep within the walls of stone,
Where cobwebs dance and gently sway,
And bats await the moon to play,
Erupts a lonely yearning moan.

The catacombs were lined with mold
And cellar rats would greedily gnaw
Discarded parts, cadavers raw
From very young to very old.

The lab was filled with beakers of brains,
Aquariums with severed limbs
And body parts from hers and hims,
And stench was stark of human remains.

But chains and pulleys amidst the death
Would hoist and jolt and surge and spark,
Defying God, aligned with Dark
To seek reversal from last breath.

Awakened from eternal rest;
The jigsaw, pieced-together thing,
Assembled part-to-part in jest,
Felt the first electric sting.

And breath filled lungs and blood coursed veins,
And pain filled heart and loss filled brains

That formed from parts, the monster's mind
That knew his soul—he'd never find.

No surgeon nor a scientist
Can make the magic light return;
For once it leaves the host, cistern,
The light goes searching for others missed.

And in that lab, the human thing,
In envy of humanity,
Sought ever means his death to bring
Without success or sanity.

G IS FOR GARGOYLE

"Mere" waterspouts at Notre Dame?
We once belonged to another race,
But even stone, we *are* not calm–
Just gaze into this monstrous face:

A dragon beast, remember me?
A thorny toad, remember me?
A ghoulish dreg, remember me?
We all were nightmares scarily.

But here in stone, we save your souls,
Protecting you and guarding those
Who venture in through hallowed doors
To sit in boats and wait for oars.

Remove the pennies from your eyes.
Give Charon his coins, the payment's due.
He'll ferry you 'cross like each who dies
But don't forget protector's who:

Remained on guard against the night,
The time of darkling predators,
And staved off countless causes of fright
From goblins, crooks and senators.

H IS FOR HALLOWEEN

"All Hallow's Eve" is Halloween.
The thirty-first is seldom seen
As simply an October day,
Despite the clouds so dark & grey.

The orange-black, a pumpkin's paint,
Inspires brows to arch–that quaint
And curious look of wonder, awe
Of nature's night of tooth & claw.

When ghosts and witches, goblins, ghouls,
Encroach allowed to test the fools
Who think they don't exist today,
Who think they might have lost their way.

They find the path back home each year;
For just one night, to thrive from fear
Instilled in those who venture out,
And knock on doors, and give the shout.

So those of you who dare to roam
Away from safety of your home
To spend the night of trick or treat
On roads where one may see & meet–
    a nightmare haunt, a scary thing,
    a shadow stark, a leather wing
Beware of what may *seem* unreal…
You'll know it from the scream you feel.

I is for Indifference

In 1964,
St. Kitty pled for more.
The lookers on ignored
Which everyone deplored.

The scumbag sprang with knife in hand,
And she complied with his demand.
Despite her doing as was told,
She felt the knife and then the cold.

The scumbag left her there to die;
There was not one…reason why.

Within the courtyard box, she saw
The witnesses who stared in awe.
She pled and bled and screamed and wept.
To her assistance, no one leapt.

Instead they drowned the noise with twists
Of volume knobs from shaking fists;
Or pulled the shades so they'd avoid
The lethal screams that so annoyed.

Eventually, to stifle pleas
The scumbag dropped her to her knees.
He finished what he started when
He tried returning to his den.

And Kitty died from wounds sustained
and yet the cause of death remained
Preventable–and yet the cure
Entails a curs'd and unknown lure.

The question most profound is this:
Why/how could they opt to miss
The chance to circumvent her need?
Instead they simply let her bleed.

I sing a hymn to Kitty, gone
A saint who died, to praise in song.
I have no words to comfort those
Who sat in silent, mute repose.

NOTE: In 1964, Kitty Genovese was stabbed to death in a courtyard in the Kews Garden District of NYC. As she lay dying, pleading for help from the neighbors in the courtyard, people turned up their radios and TVs to drown out the disturbance, some drew their window shades. Because of all the noise Kitty was making while screaming for help, the assailant returned and finished the job. Kitty was murdered while hundreds turned their backs. They were indifferent.

J IS FOR JACK-O-LANTERN

A scream is heard–it tilts its head.
A corpse is still–it widens smile.
A trick-or-treat–it glows more fierce.

Alive or dead, the pumpkin head
Observes the night in its own style;
Its eyes both seek the dark and pierce

The passersby with thoughts of dread,
Imposing scenes so bleak and vile,
That skeptics can't withhold their fears.

K IS FOR KKK

Like ghosts they ride,
Like cowards, hide
Beneath their sheets
Disguising feats
Of shame and hate
Like cruelty's mate
Against all those
Whom they oppose
Because they're born:
A jew to scorn,
A black to hang;
This killing gang
Whose mission read,
"Non-whites: Be Dead."

They say they're "knights" of ku klux klan
But honor's not a part of their plan.

The irony,
It seems to me,
Is how they cloak
These inbred folk
In hoods & sheets
Like dunce-cap geeks
  & pinhead goons
  & psycho loons.

L IS FOR LEECH

Engorged, extended sucking thing,
Vampiric worm, a slimy tube,
A parasite all black and ringed
That let's saliva be its lube

To pierce the flesh and latch its head
Until the teeth go sinking deep;
It fills its gut 'til black looks red
And cares not once if you should weep.

It dangles, hangs–don't brush it off
Or try to pull the body out–
The head dislodges coming off
And deeper eats an inside route

Until the head becomes a seed
Where others sprout just like a weed.

M IS FOR MRS. MUCKPOOL

The third-grade class will never forget
The substitute who spent the day.
Her name was Mildred Muckpool yet,
She asked that she be called *The Way*.

She spoke aloud the strangest words,
As if she prayed to gods long dead.
Although this might sound quite absurd,
She talked to, heard her cat named, "Red."

(That might not be
Curiosity…
Except her cat
Was nowhere at
The class that day.
Anyhow, anyway…)

The teacher for the day then said,
"I want a picture—something dead:
A toy, a pup, a thing now gone.
A yearned for love, a loss, a wrong."

So Megan thought and fretted blue;
She raised her hand and braved the nod;
She asked the Muckpool for a clue:
"Just why are witches feared by God?"

The Muckpool sighed, and then she grinned.
She look and knew that every eye
Then held her fast, as if she'd sinned,
And Muckpool had to tell them why.

"*Just why are witches feared by God?*"
She paused, and then, "*We witches are*
So feared, misunderstood, and odd.
But only men fear who we are.

It is the only Earthly faith
Of growth, of life, of spells, and health–
Not one views satan as more than wraith;
But still the need to use White Stealth."

And Megan knew she'd never seen
A witch so beautiful as her;
Most substitutes were wartly green,
But Muckpool caused a stunning stir.

Then Muckpool once again then said,
"*I want a picture–something dead:*
A toy, a pup, a thing now gone.
A yearned for love, a loss, a wrong."

So Megan drew a flower there:
The one she planted years ago.

And when she came back home, she stared
Upon the sight where long ago
She'd planted daisies, hoped they'd grow.
But frost had other plans and bared
The soil that naught would grow...
And there she stood and stared...

And as she looked, she saw a sprout.
The daisy seed was coming out.
What Muckpool said was coming true.
How did she know?
Where was her clue?

N IS FOR NAZI

More brutal than the Frankenstein…
More cunning than Count Dracula…
More fiendish than some poisoned wine…
More deadly than the ebola…

Another time, another place:
They started prankster-like, without a face,
They shattered glass on Kristal Nacht,
And afterwards appeared as shocked.

Imagine walking home one night,
And suddenly, the shadows sprang.
And four to one, they picked a fight
And you alone would face a gang.

Because your hair just wasn't blond;
Because your eyes just were not blue;
Because their gene pool (stagnant pond)
Had said a rat was like a jew.

And so they trampled, stomped, and bashed;
They kicked and gouged, and cut and gashed;
And left you bleeding, asking "why?"–

They didn't care if you should die.
They didn't care, but worse than that:
They thrilled, enjoyed, took pleasure from
Inflicting harm on innocence
Without the means for justice served,

Your family walks for miles;
To where the cattle cars await;

Arrival means you're packed to sate
The hungry train until it smiles.

Imagine standing hours and breath
Remains impaired until the death
Of one packed in who slips to be
The rotting carpet growingly.

Imagine when the train lets out,
The soldiers armed just scream and shout;
And if you ache and move too slow,
A bullet in your heart will glow.

Imagine then your Mom & Dad,
Too old to work the factory floor,
To enter *there*: a shower door
Where Zyklon-B's the latest fad;
They'll say a cleansing's all that waits,
"Delousing jews exacerbates."

Imagine that–from forty-one
To forty-five, how life was run;
But over yet? It'd just begun
For those who lived to see more fun.

Imagine days in camps with hope:
A laughing spectre, mocking ghost.
Arbeit macht Frei, the motto read:
The truth was: "exit only dead."

Imagine this–imagine why:
The nightmare is historic fact.
And this is where my tears impact
Upon my bias & questions why.

O IS FOR OGRE

The name "Christine" was etched in stone
Outside her cave of rocks and bones.

The bulging eyes would scan the lair
In which she'd groom her matted hair

With scratchy tongue that dripped with drool
And crumbs that reeked of ancient stool.

Out from her back, the tufts would lilt,
Like mop braids bogged with age-old guilt.

Her brow protruded, forehead sloped;
Her armpit hair was often groped

In search of lice or fleas or ticks
Or other tasty critter-licks.

The cave was fragrant, packed with smell,
Like B.O., urine, diaper hell.

The tyrant ogre grinned content,
Then farted from posterior vent.

And no one ventured there to pry.
So she'd just fester, belch and lie

Amidst her filth alone with warts
And crystal boogers like green quartz.

P IS FOR POLTERGEIST

"Or maybe it was just the wind?"
She said about the glow unskinned
That ricocheted, first left, then high,
Then paused as if to ponder why
Before it slammed the oaken door
And smashed a plate upon the floor.

If only she'd dig the basement spot
Beneath which still his body rots,
She'd find the evidence to prove
Injustice and the awful truth:
A murdered boy whose Uncle said,
"He musta run off, weren't right innis head."

That Uncle met his fate deserved;
That glow had made him more unnerved
With words in blood on mirror's glass.
The sodomy secrets would harass
His sanity each passing night,
Until a blade cut out his light.

The sheriff's auction sold the house,
But nightly after lights were doused,
The passersby would call the cops:
"A prowler's candle glows and hops,
Then dashes off through all the rooms…
Could be that runaway who zooms."

A woman bought the place, although
The neighbors spoke of eerie glows.
She moved right in with camera crews
And hoped to film unearthly news
About a soul tormented here

Who cried for someone just to hear.

The poltergeist appeared one night
When only she could see the light.
A boy of twelve with bluish glow,
With teary eyes so filled with woe,
Regret, and fear, her heart was filled;
And yet her pulse was quick and thrilled.

"I didn't run away," he said.
"I know," said she, "the papers read
That no one found a single clue
To prove you'd ever fled or flew."
The boy then said, *"My uncle was
A pedophile...I died because..."*

"He killed you." *"Yes,"* he said and then
He told her all of how and when.
But next he made a deal with her:
*"I'll let you film but what things were
Must never come...into light."*
She wondered how could things be right?

And they agreed. She filmed the glow.
But how was she to ever know?
This boy would spend eternity
Uncovered lacking sanctity.
She broke her deal, unearthed his grave,
Revealed the truth and hoped to save:

The earthbound soul she loved and knew;
She set him free—to light, he flew.
She wept and screamed. She mourned and bled
The child she lost whom she thought dead,
Because her brother would not appall...
She was his mother afterall.

Q IS FOR QUARANTINE

Contagious disease that spreads with ease
Each time he breathes the exhale means
That breath is death as black as fleas
And so they call it quarantine.

In isolation, there he lays:
Alone, untouched; already dead?
The hours in thoughts unsparked in haze
As walls all white are in his head.

All color's gone, a void, a blank;
No stimulus, it's in between.
Where once were heights and joys, it sank
To depths, not dead, and not serene.

The hell is like an elevator
That stops and lingers in the shaft,
Eternally a hesitator;
There was a time, he might have laughed.

But in between, one fear remains:
He's been assured, he'll live for years
Imprisoned like a petri stain.
No end or respite–only tears.

R IS FOR RAVEN

Have you seen the fields perhaps?
Blackened wings await the dead;
Feeding on cadavers lapsed,
Plucking eyes from corpse's head.

It's not a pretty sight to see
And Edgar Allan Poe was right
To use the Raven, meant to be
A metaphor of hopeless plight:

No chance to be atoned;
And Lazarus was stoned;
And every sin, its wrath;
As ravens sit and caw and laugh.

S IS FOR STALKER

So harmlessly, it starts benign.
So scarce a hint or sense or sign;
The subtly, a strategy,
Foreshadowing an elegy.

With frequency defying chance,
You catch a glimpse, a sight, a glance,
And wonder why the eyes don't show
The mirror of the heart or soul.

Then corners break the nervous sweat.
Then darkness sounds like breath, regret.
Then shadows coil back into night.
Suspicions thrive on nurtured fright.

And habits change, like walks alone
Or feeling safe when you're at home,
When eyes surround and penetrate
The feelings that exacerbate.

Your privacy's a yearned-for loss
And panic stains at such a cost,
For once a freedom held, now gone,
Becomes a longing, sad, sad song.

And all of this, the stalker knows,
Delighting in this cause, morose.
It feeds the thirst for fear and pain:
A sadist's thrill, an evil game.

T IS FOR TORTURE

"A Jew or Witch = both heretics,"
Declared the church by men of God
And by their candles' holy wicks,
They sentenced death with just a nod.

The Inquisition sought to save
Non-Catholic souls from flames of hell;
A noble effort–yet the graves
Were filled with tortured ones who fell.

The Inquisition gave no choice:
Confess to heresy then burn
(But not until the tortured noise
Of screams that proved the lessons learned).

Confessions signed by broken hands;
Then led to stakes, the pyre lit;
The bodies blazed, the flames were fanned
By priestly prayers, ironic wit.

I read that Jesus taught to love,
Yet in His name such acts were done.
They claimed it came from God above,
The Holy Ghost and God's own Son.

What arrogance such power must breed
Corrupting sacred Word to bleed
The innocent who wronged no one
And blame a man they call His son.

U IS FOR UNAPPRECIATED

His name was Cliff
And he was there.
No matter what–
Always there.

A tree-stuck cat, his ladder came…
The baseball lost, he saved the game…
A drowning boy, he plunged right in…
For anyone: *Samaritan*.

Imagine the shock,
The grief, dismay,
The day that Cliff
Just went away.

It seemed absurd;
He said not a word
That day that Cliff
Jumped off a cliff.

[with thanks to Edward Arlington Robinson]

V IS FOR VAMPIRE

Velvet cape, a ruby ring,
Spike-heeled boots, the satin cling,
Leather garb, and hungry smile,
Give the hints of lustful style.

She loves the night;
Her skirt is tight;
Her bust needs hands;
…you'll answer every demand.

She's dressed in black;
Reminds you of Drac;
Mascara's thick;
…she slides her tongue a lick.

Crimson lips and raven hair,
Bone-white skin, no underwear,
Mirrors prove she isn't there.
Still you say you just don't care.

Seductress tease,
She'd love to please–
But what you'll miss
…is all *before* her kiss.

W IS FOR WEREWOLF

To sprout the fur, the fangs, the drive,
To howl each night the moon is full,
To seek the flesh, the meat alive,
To know, like tides, the lunar pull.

I'd love to have that wolfen sense,
The instinct of the pack, to know:
The sounds, the sights, the sudden tense
And still, in tune with things that show

Unheard, unseen, but somehow there;
A presence prickling neck's fine hair.

Perhaps the only thing I lack:
The taste of people as a snack;

For *IF* I could– the pang– acquire
For human flesh & blood desired,

Perhaps the plunge would follow suit
And I could be the Wolf's recruit?

X IS FOR XXX

In movies rated "R," one views:
Dismemberment of body parts;
Extermination of jews;
Extraction of still-beating hearts;
The psychokiller slashing teens;
The zombie feasting on the brains;
The favorite fiends of magazines;
The act resulting in blood stains;
The alien who slaughters staff;
The child molester finding prey;
The rapist with the dark blue laugh;
The earthly scum who get away.

In movies rated triple "X,"
We view the carnal lust, desire,
The passion, craving touch through sex.
…just human beings who love the fire:
We view two people making love.
But raters place this notched above
The violence and the senseless slaughter
Of victims—each could be your daughter.

Y IS FOR YES

When death comes knocking at my door,
Is it the end or is there more?

What if I want to choose "Plan B,"
An alternate eternity?

Instead of following the light,
Is my soul more like a kite
Connected to what holds the string,
A person, place, belovèd thing?

May I then stay on Earth as ghost
Residing as a phantom host?

Must I then wait until I'm there
Before I learn if I'll still care
About the earthly thing for which
I chose "Plan B" and made the switch?

Will I remain an earthbound kite
Until I find the means to right
The wrong, the love, obsessive thing,
Until I cut umbilical string?

"Brains...Brains...Brains..."
The hunger makes them mad,
The walking dead, insane;
But are the zombies sad?

Each corpse again alive;
The rotting flesh decays;
But every step, they strive
For respite from the haze
Of cause of pain, the craze,
The satisfaction drive,
The method of their ways,
The madness twice alive.

What would I feel? What would I do?
With my soul away, my shell anew?

"Remember when I was a teen?
I couldn't say...what did I mean?
I lived inside, cocoon until
A butterfly became my will:
A monarch, orange, black,
Like nights of Halloween;
But once there was a lack
Until cocoon's age of teen:
A metamorphosis becomes
A transfer like this zombie shell;
Remember me, despite what numbs,
The day will come when all is well..."

To stop the dead–undead
Requires buckshot in the head.
The trigger's primed,
Your finger's timed,
But will you put him back to bed?

Clement was born in Pittsburgh and raised in Mentor (an eastside suburb of Cleveland).

In 1980, he joined the U.S. Army. He enlisted for the 1st Ranger Battalion in Savannah. Clement became airborne, Ranger, pathfinder, jungle expert, and expert infantry. In June of 1983, Clement went to his second duty assignment in West Berlin. He was assigned to the Scout platoon of 2nd Battalion, 6th Infantry. They patrolled the Berlin Wall in the American sector with live ammo and two gun jeeps. Clement moved to Florida in 2004 where he met Lynn. Lynn and Clement became community association managers. They now live in Estero with two cats: Chatanooga choo choo McGoo and Tatchmo Vagabound.